Chatty Cat
My Purr-fect Friends

Suzan Collins

With best wishes
Suzan x

Published by East Anglian Press

Copyright © Suzan Collins 2016

The right of Suzan Collins to be identified as author
of this work has been asserted in accordance with
the Copyright, Designs and Patents Act 1988.

British Library Cataloguing in Publication Data.
A CIP catalogue record for this book is available
from the British Library.

ISBN: 978-0-9934934-5-4

Acknowledgements:

Emily Hummel, Megan Hummel and Ruby Ashman for their cat stories.

Katie Phillips, Mary Purtill, Anne Earley, Rachel Lawston, Reymen Miah and Jo Wilde for their animal pictures.

Jo Wilde for permission to use collar tree idea and Natalie Davison for permission to use Paws for Thought

Jo Wilde: Editing
Lynne Rooney: Book illustrations
Rachel Lawston: Cover creation

Thank you for reading my books and coming to my book signings. I love telling you about Chatty Cat.
Reading is very good for you. Keep reading!

Chatty Cat
My Purr-fect Friends

Suzan Collins

Contents

Introduction

Chatty Cat: My Purr-fect Friends is the third book in a series of Chatty Cat books about the life of a rescue cat having a happy time and meeting new friends.

If you are looking for an animal, whether it is a cat, kitten, dog or rabbit, or any other animal, please consider adopting one from your local shelter. Many now advertise the animals needing a forever home on their Facebook page.

Happy reading,
Suzan x

Chatty Cat

Stray Cat

Clancy Cat

Toffee Cat

Bert the Parrot

Sooty Cat

Om and Daenerys the Tortoises

Brandi Dog & Rocky Dog

Preface

I was a stray and had been in a pen, in a cat shelter. They called me Twinkle. I was there for three months.

I moved in to my new home in 2013 and I am very happy here. This is my fur-ever home. I talk a lot and my name was changed from Twinkle to Chatty Cat.

I am happy and I feel safe here. I have a nice bed, well quite a few beds, around my house and I am fed twice a day.

I go out a lot now so only use my toilet tray when I can't be bothered to go out, or it's too cold to go out, or the door isn't open.

I had hoped that Jade would get me a key to the door so I can go out when I want to. Well, not really a key, but a cat flap. It's the same, isn't it?

I have some scratching posts, one upstairs on the landing and one downstairs in the lounge. I scratch my claws on these instead of ruining the furniture.

I like playing with small balls. I have blue one and quite a few white ones. I hit a few of them around the lounge and into the hall, they're nice and light. My bestest toy is the small blue ball. I like the white ones but they're a bit too light and hard to tame.

I have a blue collar with a bell on it and a disc with Jade's phone number on it. She couldn't put my phone number on it because I haven't got a phone. Jade likes this collar because the bell will warn the birds I am here and the collar will open if it gets caught on a branch.

Some of the things I like:

Company - don't leave me alone for too long.
People stroking the top of my head or under my chin.
Playing (when I want to).
The sun on my back.
Sitting in my jungle.
Peace and quiet.

Some of the things I don't like:

Loud noises- thunder, fireworks, motorbikes.
People chasing me.
People standing over me (like giants).
Having my claws clipped.
Stroking my back (unless I am sat on your lap).

Love

Chatty Cat

xx

It's Summer

I am sitting on the bedroom windowsill and the sun switch is on. The sun is shining in on me and I am lovely and warm. I am waiting for Jade to wake up. She's been in MY bed for ages. Yes it is MY bed but I let Jade sleep in it too.

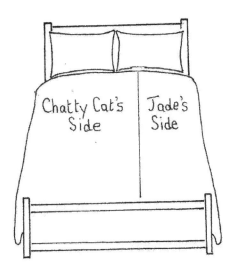

I look out of the window and see two big white seagulls on the grass. They are huge! Well not huge huge but a lot bigger than me.

I meow to them, 'Make some of your loud noises and wake Jade up purrlease*' But they cannot hear me, the window is too thick. I turn my head and look over at Jade sleeping, willing her to wake up, but she doesn't. I jump from the windowsill onto the bed. Thud!

*Purrlease is a Chatty Cat word for please.
You pronounce it Purr-lease!

I look her way and see that she is awake but she is not talking. I know that when she talks it means she's getting up and I'll get some food.

I'm not hungry but if she is going to give me some food I'm not going to say no.

Jade stretches in the bed. 'Hello Chatty Cat,' she says. I meow 'Hello,' and walk up the bed to her so she can stroke me twice on the head, and when she's done that I turn a little so she can stroke my back twice then I stroll to the edge of the bed and jump down onto the floor.

She gets out of bed and walks into the bathroom and closes the door before I can get in there. I meow, 'Jade, you've closed the door and I can't get in.' She doesn't answer and I look up at the door handle waiting for it to move. When the handle does move the door opens and I quickly run in and see what she has been hiding from me. I walk around the floor of the bathroom and cannot see anything different. So why, why, why did she close the door? Silly shehooman* Jade.

She runs down the stairs and I run down too, faster than her because I need to get to the kitchen first, to sit by my food dishes and meow, 'Can I have my food purrlease?' She puts my food down and makes her own breakfast. I know this without watching what she's doing because she does it every morning, and I mean *every* morning. She's just switched the kettle on and now she is walking through the house and will open the back door. Then she will come back and finish making her breakfast. Anyway, enough of her, I've just finished eating my food and I can smell my food over by Jade... oh, hang on a minute, what is she doing? I jump up onto the stool and watch her. She's putting MY meat and MY biscuits on a plate. But it's not MY plate.

* Shehooman is a Chatty Cat word for a lady.
  You pronounce it she-hooman!

I watch her walk out of the kitchen and close the door. Not again!

Twice now she has left me behind a door. How can I see what's going on if she keeps doing this? I hear her footsteps coming close to the door and I look up at the door handle. I see it turning and when the door opens I run to the back of the house to the back door. I stop abruptly, not only can I smell cat, but I can see a black and white one, well really it's a white cat with black patches. In MY garden-room! What the heck?! I run into the garden-room to shoo it away and it runs under the gate and out of MY garden-room. Phew! I'm out of breath, I'm sure it's due to the hot sun. I walk slowly up the path, panting all the way. I walk into the house and go in each room to see where Jade is. I can't see her downstairs and I haven't got enough energy to run upstairs to see if she's up there so I go and sit on the carpet by the back door and look out into MY garden-room. It's nice and tidy. The grass was cut yesterday.

I have a little rest. It's really hot now. I want to ask Jade to turn the sun switch off, it's too hot now. Ah here she is coming through the front door with Jim.

'I thought you were upstairs. Where have you been?' I ask.

'Outside,' says Jade.

'In the front garden-room? Can you turn the sun switch off Jade?'

'No, I can't, Chatty Cat.'

'Purrlease.'

'No.'

'I said "Purrlease".'

'I know you did but I don't know how to switch it off.'

'Quick, follow me.'

'Where are we going?'

'Just follow me.' I run and jump up onto the table in my garden-room.

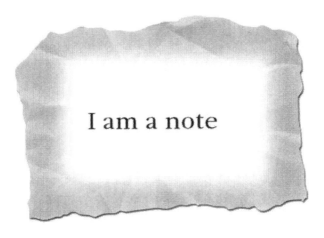

'Look, here is a note...'

'Yes but it's only a piece of paper.'

'Yes but hoomans* know everything so go and find the switch and turn it off. Purrlease. I am so hot.'

*Hoomans is a Chatty Cat word for humans.
    You pronounce it hoo-man!

Jade puts a damp towel on the floor and I look at her. 'It's to cool you down.' She says.

I lie on it and I can feel it cooling me down.

Later I walk down the path to the tree and I can smell cat again. I look to my left and I can see white cat paws underneath the gate.

Who's that in MY Garden-room?

It was really hot last night and I slept on the wooden flooring. I've just had breakfast and have left some biscuits for later.

I walk through to the back door which Jade has already opened and look out into my garden-room. 'Whoa! What are you doing here? I shooed you away yesterday.' As it walks up the path I stare at it and stand up. It's coming closer and I raise my tail to show I am upset.

It stops a few feet away from me.

'This is MY garden-room. What are you doing here? Who are you?' I ask.

'My name is Stray Cat,' the cat meows.

'You look familiar. Ah, I know you. You used to sleep on the roof of MY shed. Well, I think it's MY shed.'

'Yes I did. And it's everyone's shed.'

'Everyone's?'

'Everyone's, but no hoomans, only cats.'

'What do you want?'

'Have you got any food?'

'Only MY food. Why do you ask?'

'I'm hungry. I've been out all night.'

'Why were you out all night?'

'I always go out at night but I haven't gone home for breakfast. I decided to come here instead.'

I stare at the cat.

'So, have you got any food?' Stray Cat asks again.

'I've got some biscuits but I was saving them for later.'

'Oh, go on, let me have some. Just a few, then I will go and leave you in peace.'

'Why don't you go home and have your breakfast?'

'I can't be bothered. It's too far. Go on, let me have some.'

'I will go and see my shehooman Jade, she might give you some.'

I run into the kitchen. 'Jade, Jade, come and see, Stray Cat wants some food.'

'Stray Cat?' Jade asks.

'Yes, Stray Cat. The cat that used to sleep on top of my shed roof. He's back. Quick, come and follow me and have a look.'

Jade follows me. We walk into the garden-room, and she sees Stray Cat.

'Hello, you beauty,' Jade says to Stray Cat. 'You were here yesterday.'

Stray Cat walks up to Jade and stands still while Jade bends down and strokes him. Stray Cat is more patient than me. He stays there quite a while and lets Jade stroke him. Much longer than I do.

'He wants some food,' I meow. Jade doesn't answer. 'He wants some food,' I meow again.

'Would you like some food Stray Cat?' Jade asks.

'I just said that he did.'

Stray Cat meows, 'Yes purrlease.'

Jade goes into the house and into the kitchen. I walk quickly behind her, hoping that I'll get some food too.

Jade opens the door of the big white fridge and gets something out of it and closes the door again. I sniff. Mmmnnn... I can smell chicken. She walks over to the drawer and gets out something to scoop the meat onto a plate for Stray Cat. I sit by my dish and meow, 'Can I have some too please?'

She puts some meat on a plate and then comes over to me and puts some food onto my plate. I look at my plate and then at Stray Cat's plate.

'Stray Cat has more food than me,' I meow.

'He is more active than you and needs more food. Besides, you've already had your breakfast.'

'Are you saying that I am phat*?' I meow.

*Phat is a Chatty Cat word for fat!
  You pronounce it fat!

'No I am not. I'm just saying...' Jade says as she walks out of the kitchen with the plate of food and closes the door behind her.

Again I am left behind a door!

I meow, 'Jade, you've left me behind the door again.' She doesn't answer. I raise my right paw and tap on the door hoping it will open but it doesn't. I try and put my paw into the bottom corner of the door to open it but my paw won't fit. I am not happy and I sit by the door and sulk.

I hear Jade walking to the door and I move back a little, just enough room for her to open the door and for me to run out as quickly as I can.

Running through the house I slide on the shiny wooden floor. Wheeeeee! I get to the back door and I see Stray Cat is warming up his body on the patio.

I tiptoe past him as quietly as I can and go and sit on the bin.

I can see him from up here. I will ignore him and pretend he is not here. I wonder how he keeps the white bits of his fur so clean.

After a while Stray Cat gets up and stretches, then walks along my path and under the gate, and then he's gone.

I jump down and stroll into the house to see where Jade is and to eat the rest of my biscuits. I'll be having more soon and I must eat these up now so Jade sees my empty plate.

After I eat them I stroll into the lounge and gently tap my light blue ball with my left paw so it goes under the settee. I don't want anyone taking it and it will be safe there.

Where's the smell coming from?

Jade is still asleep but I've been up for a while. I keep looking out of the window, but I can't see Stray Cat. I walk into the next room and leap up onto the windowsill. I can't see him through that window either.

I jump when I hear the trill of the clock and run in to see Jade. I bound onto the bed. 'Quick! Quick! Follow me,' I tell her. I spring off the bed and walk out onto the landing. Jade is just getting out of bed.

'Come on, hurry up,' I say.

'What's the rush, Chatty Cat?'

'Quick! Follow me,' I say as I run down the stairs. I can hear her following me. I run through the house and out to the back door. I sit there and meow. 'Quick, open the door, open the door.'

Jade places her hand on the handle and it opens. I rush through the opening out into the garden-room. I quickly look around but can't see Stray Cat. I sit on the path.

'Are you okay, Chatty Cat?' Jade asks. I give a faint meow to say, 'I'm okay,' but really I'm not. I'm sad because Stray Cat isn't here, he was good company and now he's gone. I feel all alone. Jade wouldn't understand, being a hooman. I look across my garden-room, all quiet and still.

My eyes see a ladybird on a leaf, it's wearing a red coat with black spots. I watch it climb the leaf, it stops at the top and climbs down the other side.

I can hear the familiar sound of the microwave pinging, probably Jade cooking her porridge, and it reminds me that I haven't had my breakfast yet. I walk quickly through the house and into the kitchen and meow, 'I haven't had my breakfast yet. I haven't had my breakfast yet.' I look down at my dish, 'Oh, there is my food, thank you.' I eat the meat quickly and sit down to eat the biscuits. Crunch crunch. When I finish, I stand up and look around to see if there's any more food for me. Nope! There's nothing. I stroll through the house and sit on the back of the settee whilst Jade eats her breakfast. I have a good view of her from here. The spoon clatters against the bowl as she scoops up the remaining bits of porridge. When I hear her do this sound I know it's not long before I get my share. That's if she doesn't wash the dish straight away.

I am distracted by a butterfly coming through the window. It flies around for a little while and then settles on the windowsill. I quietly and slowly tiptoe over to the window and dip my body ready to pounce at the butterfly. I am just about to jump and Jade catches the butterfly in her hands and puts it out the window. Spoilsport Jade.

Sniffing the fresh air coming through the window, I decide to go over and climb through it and walk along the ledge. Jade opens the other window and I walk back in through this window. I jump down onto the carpet and walk out of the back door into the garden-room. The path is warm and I jump up onto the bin and warm my bottom.

It's not long before I can smell food. It's far away but I can just about smell it. I jump up onto the garden gate and sniff again.

The smell isn't any stronger up here and I have to make a decision of walking a long way to find this food or staying here and waiting for my next feed. I decide to stay here. I climb down onto the path which is still lovely and warm, and I throw myself down onto it. I stretch my body out so the heat warms up my tummy and when it is lovely and warm I lie on my side and fall asleep.

Magpie Birds

Stray Cat and I are sitting on the bin when we hear noises, noises of birds telling other birds to get away from their nests.

We stop chatting and jump down onto the grass, lower our bodies under the gate, and run down the path. The birds need our help and we run as fast as we can. When we get to the thick tree trunk we sit and look up at the tree. It's r-e-a-l-l-y big and r-e-a-l-l-y high.

I wonder if I can climb that high. I'm sure Stray Cat can because he is a phit* cat, but I'm not. I don't do a lot of exercise. I look over at Stray Cat and watch as he leaps onto the tree trunk and climbs up the tree. The birds are still making noises. I look up through the big branches and can just about see a black and white magpie bird. I hope he doesn't want to eat the little birds in the nest but I think he does cos that's what magpie birds do.

I hear a lot of rustling up there. I hope Stray Cat has scared the magpie bird away. I know it's nature for magpie birds to eat little birds but it makes me unhappy.

Oooh, look. The magpie bird is flying away. And I watch as Stray Cat walks proudly down the big tree trunk.

'Well done, Stray Cat. You really should be called Super Cat.'

'It was nothing,' he says as he starts walking, and I follow him.

*Phit is a Chatty Cat word for fit.
   You pronounce it fit!

38

Stray Cat comes with an ASBO

I am sitting by the door and am looking out into my garden-room and I see Stray Cat walking up the path. He's got a blue round thing attached to his collar. He's now about to come into MY house.

Is it a watch? No, can't be, he wouldn't be able to see it. Is it his food tin? Perhaps it's a new container to keep his cat biscuits in when he goes for a sleepover. What a great idea. I want one. Although I don't do sleepovers, I wonder if I can still have one. I run and find Jade.

'Stray Cat has a container round his neck. Can I have one?'

'A what?'

'A container. Come and have a look.'

I walk out to the garden-room and Jade follows me.

'That's not a container, it's a tracker.'

'A what?' I asked.

'A tracker so his hehooman* knows where he is.'

'No biscuits?'

'No, Chatty Cat, no biscuits.'

I am disappointed. I flick my tail up in the air and run along the path.

'Why you running?' asks Stray Cat.

'So Jade can't catch me. I don't want a tracker on my collar. Or an ASBO.'

* Hehooman is a Chatty Cat word for a man. You pronounce it he-hooman!

'An ASBO?'

'Yeah, that blue thing you've got on your collar. Jade says it's a tracker but it's an ASBO. I've seen naughty boys on the telly wearing them.'

'I don't want one either but I have no choice. My hehooman put it on me and when I go back home he takes it off and attaches it to his laptop. Hoomans are weird at times.'

'Why don't you put it on the collar tree?' I ask. 'Come on, I'll take you.'

I walk down the path and Stray Cat follows me. We lower our bodies, squeeze under the gate and walk along the path. We walk along the pavement and stop by the kerb. It's not a busy road but we still stop. We look left, then right, then left again. 'No cars. Come on, let's cross the road,' I tell Stray Cat and we cross the road to the other side. We jump onto a small wall and walk along it for a while and then we jump down onto some soft grass.

We turn left into a big garden-room, bigger than mine.

'Wow, look at all these trees,' meows Stray Cat. 'I haven't been here before.'

'Do you know what you have to do, Stray Cat?'

'Um, no.'

'Go to the collar tree over there, and rub your neck against it until your collar comes off,' I tell him.

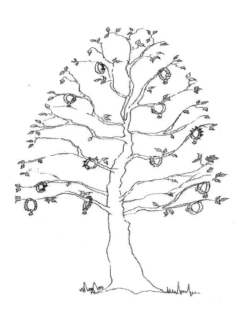

'And then what do I do?'

'You pick up the collar in your mouth and hang it on one of the branches.'

A small black cat is walking towards us.

'Hello Stray Cat, haven't seen you here before. Why have you got an ASBO attached to your collar?'

'See, told you it was an ASBO.' I said. 'Who are you?'

'I'm Sooty Cat.'

'That's it, I've had enough,' said Stray Cat as he walks towards the tree. I watch him climb a little way up the tree, he does it really quickly. He walks along a thick branch and rubs his neck on the big branch, and after some more rubbing the collar comes off and falls to the ground. Sooty Cat runs to the collar and picks it up then Sooty Cat climbs the tree and hangs it on a branch.

'Okay to hang it here, Stray Cat?'

'Anywhere, I don't mind,' said Stray Cat. And he watches as Sooty Cat hangs it on the branch. Stray Cat sits and scratches his right ear with his right paw before climbing back down the tree, with Sooty Cat following him, digging their claws into the bark of the tree so they do not slip.

Stray Cat lies on the grass and washes himself, and Sooty lies nearby. I decide to go home and be fussed over by Jade.

I meow, 'I'm home' when I get into the garden-room and see Jade and Jim sat having a drink. Soon she will prepare my food. Wonder what I am having?

Going for a walk

The sun switch is on and the sun is shining through the window. I can see Stray Cat in the Cat Den in my garden-room.

I'm waiting for Jade to open the door. I try and open it myself but it won't open.

When Jade opens the door I sit on the mat and look at Stray Cat. He stretches out his body and walks up to me.

'I've been waiting in your garden-room for a while. What took you so long? I went and had a sleep whilst I was waiting,' says Stray Cat.

'I had to wait for Jade to open the door,' I tell Stray Cat.

'Got any food?' asks Stray Cat.

'I've just eaten mine. It's only Friday, you usually come at the weekend,' I tell him.

'I know it's Friday. Friday is the new Caturday*. Got any food?' Stray Cat asks again.

'Will you be sleeping on my roof later?'

'It's not your roof. I told you, it belongs to all cats.'

'Let's call it the cat roof.' I say.

*Caturday is a Chatty Cat word for Saturday. You pronounce it Cat-ur-day!

'Okay. It's lovely and sunny. Got any food?' Stray Cat asks for the third time.

'Give me some food and I'll tell you if I am going to sleep on the cat roof later. Or... I may go back home,' Meows Stray Cat.

Jade comes out into the garden-room and talks to Stray Cat. 'Hello lovely boy,' she says and bends down to stroke him. He bangs his head into her legs and Jade strokes him again. 'I guess you'd like some food. I'll go and get you some.' And off Jade goes back into the house. It isn't long before she comes back out with two plates of food, one being bigger than the other. Jade puts the biggest plate in front of Stray Cat and the smaller one by me. I don't mind him having the biggest plate. I'm quite full from earlier.

I finish mine and watch Stray Cat eat his and when he's finished I watch him lick his lips. Looks like he really enjoyed that.

'You fancy a walk, Chatty Cat?' Stray Cat asks.

'I was going to jump up onto one of the bins and have a sleep.'

'Come on, let's go for a walk.'

'Okay, I could do with some exercise instead of sleeping all the time. I don't want to get phat.'

'Why are you talking about, 'phat'?'

'I hear some of the mums by the school gates saying they don't want to get phat and their little children say that they don't want to get phat either.'

'Mums shouldn't be talking like that in front of little children cos they may grow up worrying about it and then they'll have health problems.'

'That's what I thought. It's wrong, isn't it?'

'Yes it is. Don't ever talk of phat again. Come on.'

I follow Stray Cat and when he jumps up onto the first wall, I do too. We walk along the top, a bit narrow but enough room for our paws.

'I come this way often,' he said, turning back to me.

'Do you?'

'Yes! I just said I did,' Stray Cat said, before walking on a few more steps and then stopping. 'Come on, let's jump down here.'

'Why? Is there any food down there?' I ask.

'No.'

'So why are we going to jump all the way down there onto the grass?'

'It's not far.'

'It is.'

'Come on, I want to show you something.'

Stray Cat jumps down and then I jump down to join him. My paws land on the grass and I follow Stray Cat who is walking towards a window. I watch him jump up onto the ledge and look through the window. I jump up. This feels weird as I'm usually in my house looking out of the window, not the other way around.

'This is Bert the Parrot.' Stray Cat meows.

'He's colourful,' I meow.

'Lovely colours, nice boy,' meows Stray Cat.

'Do you fancy him?'

'What?!'

'Do you fancy him?' I repeated.

'I heard you the first time. No I don't fancy him, he's a bird and I'm a cat. Duh! I like his red beak and light blue head, much prettier than the pigeons,' Stray Cat meows.

'What about the big white seagulls?' I ask.

'What about them?' Stray Cat says.

'Do you like them, too?'

'I have to, they are so big,' Stray Cat says and I agree with him.

'What happens now?' I ask.

'Usually Bert comes to the window and says hello, but look, he's busy with the phone at the moment.'

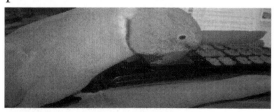

'Let's go and see if Om and Daenerys are out,' Stray Cat meows.

'What are they?' I meow to Stray Cat.

'Tortoises,' Stray Cat meows back.

'Tortoises? Is that the round animals with legs?'

'Yes, and they're my friends, come on,' Stray Cat says as he jumps up on the wall.

'Okay, wait for me.' And I jump up and follow him.

It takes us a long time to walk along this wall because it has tree branches everywhere so we have to walk slowly and weave in and out of the branches. We walk a long way and my little legs are hurting. Stray Cat has long legs but I've only got short stumpy ones.

'Are we there yet?' I ask Stray Cat.

'Nearly. Keep walking.'

I sit down for a rest.

'Ooooh, look, there they are, come on,' Stray Cat says, looking down at two tortoises.

'What are they eating?' I ask Stray Cat.

'Cucumber. You don't know much, do you?'

'I know enough,' I say.

'Like what?'

'I know where to get my food and how to meow nicely so my shehooman gives me more food.'

'Who is shehooman?'

'That's my Jade.'

'So why call her shehooman?'

'Cos she's a she and she is a hooman. You don't know much, do you?'

'Mn...come on, let's jump down and see Om and Daenerys.'

I watch Stray Cat walk over to them.

'Hey, Daenerys, have you seen Charlie?'

'Charlie?' Daenerys asks.

'Yeah, you know, Charlie Mouse.'

'Ah, Charlie Mouse, saw him about ten feed times ago.'

I sit and watch them talking but I'm getting bored so I stand up and walk over to them. I sniff Daenerys, he smells funny. I sniff him again, and he still smells funny, a bit like dandelions.

'Come on Chatty Cat, we're off,' Stray Cat says.

I stand up and follow him and we walk in and out of the flowers. Stray Cat stops to sniff a leaf. I walk round the other side of the leaf and smell it. It smells like an insect has been here. Or is it a snail? I'm still thinking who or what has been on the leaf when I see Stray Cat has stopped sniffing and is walking away. I sniff a bit more and then run and catch him up.

'Phew! You walk fast,' I tell Stray Cat. He doesn't answer. He lowers his body, and then jumps and stretches up onto the wall, and I do the same. The wall is really high, about four feet, and it isn't easy to jump up onto. But I do it. When we run out of wall Stray Cat jumps onto a wooden fence, it is really wide and I don't know if I can jump it but I try and I manage it! The wooden fence is rough and it hurts my paws to walk on it, but I have no choice, I have to. I want to stay with Stray Cat. He doesn't seem to mind he just walks along the top of it. Eventually he climbs down the fence and onto the grass. I follow, oooh, so nice to have something soft under my paws I think, as I land on the grass.

I sniff, mmm... I can smell juicy meat. I follow the smell and meow to Stray Cat.

'Food. You coming?'

'Of course.'

We walk through the legs and shoes and I stop and sniff a pair of leather black shoes. I want to rub my body on them but I don't think the hooman would like it so I don't. I walk on and follow Stray Cat who is walking closer to the smell of meat. I wish they would turn the music down. I've got very good hearing and I don't need it this loud.

Stray Cat is stood by the tin thing hoomans cook food on in the garden-room. The smell is too good not to do anything. Stray Cat must feel the same as he stretches up and tries to hook a sausage with his paw.

'Get down!' shouts the man with a steel thing in his hand. 'Go on. Shoo!' I watch as Stray Cat runs away. The smell of the meat is making my mouth water and I want some but how can I do it so I don't get caught? I hide behind some legs whilst I think what to do. I'm trying to look round this white leg but the hairs are getting in the way. I look round the other side and there are hairs there too.

'Ow!' I screech as something hits my head. I hear it drop to the floor and look to see what it is. It's a sausage, but before I can do anything I hear a voice.

'Oooh look, what a cute cat,' a shehooman says. 'Would you like some food, you cutie?'

I look at her and the shiny thing hanging round her neck. I want to grab it as it shines but then I remember that there is a sausage on the floor that I want to take. Shehooman goes to stroke me and I turn, pick up the sausage and walk as fast as I can between the legs. It's not easy, there are many legs, different sizes and, oh dear, hehooman is wearing socks with his sandals. I shake my head and carry on. I would try and run but there are too many legs. Eventually there are not so many legs and I run as fast as I can until I see Stray Cat. I drop the sausage. 'Want to share?' I ask.

'Yes purrlease.'

Stray Cat starts eating one end of the sausage and I start at the other end. We are both purring as we eat and when we finish we sit and lick our lips before wetting our paws and washing around our mouths.

When we arrive near to my house Stray Cat says, 'I'm going home now.'

I meow, 'Bye,' and walk home. When I get there I go into my house and lay down on the carpet. Gosh, we walked a lot, my poor paws!

I can see my blue ball under the settee. I wonder where my white table tennis ball is and raise my head to look around the floor. Ah, there it is by the television. I lower my head back down to the floor and have a well needed sleep.

Stealing poop!

I am sleeping on the desk and I hear the rustle of my litter tray being touched. 'Oh no!' I cry, 'she's stealing my poop!' I run downstairs as fast as I can but it's too late. She's put it in a bag and is walking out to the bin. And... she has washed my toilet tray and put it outside too! I used to think that she was cleaning my tray but I heard something on the television about hoomans stealing poop.

I can see Stray Cat is on the bin, and I go over and join him. He's got his eyes closed and I wonder if he is sleeping, but even if he is, I need to wake him up and tell him about shehooman Jade stealing my poop.

'Shehooman keeps stealing my poop,' I tell Stray Cat.

'Yeah, yeah. Hoomans do it all the time,' meows Stray Cat.

'Do your Hoomans take yours?'

'Nah.'

'Why not? Is your poop not worth anything?'

'I poop where they can't get at it.'

'What shall I do? Every time my Jade steals my poop, she cleans my litter tray and when she puts clean litter stuff in there I have to quickly go and poop again so my poop is in there.'

'And then what happens?'

'She comes and steals it again.'

'You need to see Clancy.'

'Who is Clancy?'

'Clancy runs the Poop Group. I'll take you there tomorrow evening.'

The Poop Group

Stray Cat and I stroll into the room and see a bird perched on a table.

'Hello Stray Cat,' squawks Bert the Parrot.

'Hello Bert, still got the phone with you I see,' Stray Cat says to him.

'Chatty Cat, this is Clancy Cat, he's the leader of the group,' says Stray Cat.

'Hello. Clancy Cat, I like your ginger coat.' He doesn't answer and just stares at me.

He's sat on a table which is fine but... he's wearing glasses.

'Stray Cat said I should come here to ask why my shehooman Jade keeps stealing poop out of my toilet tray.'

'You've come to the right place. Let me close the door first so hoomans don't hear us.'

'Now, how much poop does your shehooman steal?' asks Clancy Cat.

'One or two round ones a day,' I meow back.

'What litter is in your tray?'

'Sometimes it's the fluffy white stuff and other times it's the clumping stuff. What do you use?'

'I like my shehooman Mary to use the wooden stuff,' said Clancy Cat.

'Does she use it all the time?' I ask Clancy Cat.

'She does now. She used to use different stuff but I told her I didn't like it.'

'Does she steal your poop?' I ask Clancy Cat.

'Yeah she does, but I don't want it.'

'I don't want my poop either,' squawks Bert the Parrot.

'My shehooman steals my poop too,' says one of the torts.

'There are a lot of hooman thieves out there. What are we going to do, Clancy Cat?'

Clancy Cat thought for a moment.

'Can you hold it in until you go outside?' asks Clancy Cat.

'Sometimes I can, but what about when I have my duvet days?'

'Duvet days?' asks Clancy Cat.

'Yes, the days when I sleep on top of the duvet.'

'All day?'

'Of course, usually on a Monday and sometimes on a Wednesday,' I say.

'If you're asleep all day when do you poop?'

'When I hear Jade's car pull up I run downstairs into my en suite and poop.'

'En suite?' asks Clancy Cat.

'It's my toilet room. I have my toilet tray, cat litter and scoop in it.'

'Why don't you man up and go outside to poop?' asks Clancy Cat.

'Because I am a lady,' I tell Clancy Cat.

Chatty Cat learns something

I am eating my breakfast in the kitchen and Stray Cat is eating his by the door. I eat my food quickly as I want to ask Stray Cat what we are doing today.

When I finish my meat I eat some of my biscuits and go out into my garden-room. I watch as Stray Cat comes out. He sits and licks his right paw and washes his face. He does it four times before coming over to me and asking, 'You coming?'

'Where you going?' I ask.

'To the Feed-Me-Now-Group.'

'The Feed-Me-Now-Group?'

I ask. 'What's that?'

'We talk about ways we can get our hoomans to feed us when we want to be fed and not when they want to feed us.'

'That sounds a good idea. Yes, I'm coming.'

Stray Cat and I walk along the path, jump up onto the wall and down the other side. We walk along the grass until we come across a large umbrella and see Bert the Parrot, Sooty Cat and another cat.

'Who is this?' I whisper to Stray Cat.

'Chatty Cat this is Toffee Cat.'

'Nice to meet you, Toffee Cat.' I say.

'And nice to meet you, Chatty Cat.'

'I don't like it when my shehooman throws a pretend mouse for me to catch. Is she saying that she wants me to bring her home a mouse?' says Sooty Cat. 'Because I can.'

'I don't like it when my shehooman keeps saying, 'I know, I know,' every time I meow at her, because she doesn't know, does she?' says Toffee Cat.

'She might know,' I say. 'Jade knows what I am saying.'

'Does she? Does she?' says Sooty Cat.

'Of course she does. Doesn't she, Stray Cat?' I look at Stray Cat waiting for him to answer. But he doesn't.

'I thought this was the Feed-Me-Now-Group not the Does-My-Hooman-Understand-What-I am-Saying-Group,' says Toffee cat.

'It is,' squawks Bert the Parrot.

'Where you living tonight, Stray Cat?' says Clancy Cat.

'I'm staying in the Cat Den in Chatty Cat's garden-room,' says Stray Cat. 'Are you going somewhere for a sleep over, or going home to your hooman, Clancy Cat?'

Clancy Cat lies down and says, 'Going home. My shehooman has been at work all day and will be home with some treats for me.'

'Why's that?'

'I make her feel guilty for going out to work and leaving me home alone, and she buys me treats.'

'But you're not left at home alone. You are out with us,' says Bert the parrot, stating the obvious.

'I know that, but she doesn't.'

'You better get home before she does then,' squawks Bert the Parrot.

'I know that too,' says Clancy Cat.

'I'm going home. The football is on tonight and I don't want to miss it,' says Bert the Parrot.

'I like to watch The Simpsons,' I say.

'I'm too busy out walking and visiting people and haven't got time to watch TV,' says Stray Cat.

'I don't watch TV but I like to sit on the fence when the sun switch is on.' says Toffee Cat.

Clancy Cat raises his head, 'Sooty Cat, when you get old will your black fur turn grey, like it does with old people?'

Sooty answers, 'I don't know. I am not old yet.'

'That was funny! That was funny!' chirps Bert the Parrot as he dances on top of the umbrella.

'It wasn't that funny,' says Clancy Cat.

Bert the Parrot stops dancing and says, 'It was. You didn't find it funny because you haven't got your glasses on.'

I lay on the grass with Stray Cat, Toffee Cat, Clancy Cat and Sooty Cat. It's lovely and quiet. A young boy walks past with his mummy and all us cats lift our heads to make sure he walks straight past us and when he does, we lower our heads again.

'I'm hungry,' chirps Bert the Parrot.

'Me too,' says Toffee Cat.

'And me,' I say. 'I had yellow fish the other day.'

'What, on Fish-Friday?' asks Sooty Cat.

'I can't remember what day it was, it was yellow fish not white fish like I usually have on Fish-Friday.' I say.

'So it was Fish-Friday then?' says Sooty Cat.

We rest our heads on the ground, there's a few stony things touching my fur and I don't like it. I stand up and walk a few paces and then lie down again. It's all quiet until Stray Cat gets up and stretches his long body... 'Come on Chatty Cat, it's Feed-Me-Now time.'

I stand up and stretch out my front paws and then my back ones.

'It's my Feed-Me-Now time too,' says Toffee Cat as she stands up and stretches her front paws then her back ones.

Strolling up my garden-room path I ask Stray Cat, 'When would the group have discussed Feed-Me-Now-Time? We discussed everything else.'

'Do we really need to discuss it?'

'Of course. Why not?'

'Because cats are in charge and the hoomans are our slaves. Just meow until your hooman/slave feeds you when you want to be fed.'

A walk with Toffee Cat

Jade has just put some food into the microwave so I'm waiting, waiting for her to cook her food and give me some. She doesn't usually give me food at lunchtime unless I meow, and meow, and meow when she takes the food out of the microwave. Or when I walk round her feet and in and out of her legs so some food drops onto the floor. I'll just throw myself onto the kitchen floor right here and wait for the microwave to ping.

Oooh look, I'm in kitchen prison. Not really, it's the sun coming through the window.

'Chatty, you're sitting right in the middle of the kitchen. Now I have to step over you,' says Jade.

'I know. I'm here so you don't forget me,' I meow. 'I smell Tuna, can I have some?'

'Wait and see.'

'Wait and see? Why can't you tell me now?' She doesn't answer.

I lie quietly and wait for the microwave to ping.

PING! sounds the microwave, and I stand up and meow. I meow all the time whilst she is putting the food onto a plate. I'm too small to see up onto the counter and if I jump up there she'll only tell me to get down so I'm saving my energy. I hear the familiar sound of a saucer being taken off the pile which means I am going to get some food. I walk over to my mat and meow until food is put down for me. I meow,

'Thank you' and eat it, and then I walk through the house and out into the garden-room, down the path, under the gate and along the path.

'Ooh, is that Toffee Cat?' I ask myself. I only see shadows but I have a great smell and I sniff, yep, that's Toffee Cat. I walk over to her.

'Hello Toffee Cat,' I say to her.

'Hello Chatty Cat. Where are you going?'

'I don't know. Just fancied an afternoon stroll. What are you doing?'

'I'm sitting down,' says Toffee Cat, stating the obvious. 'Are you going far? I don't want too much exercise today.'

'My shehooman Jade was telling the telephone that two dogs have moved in.'

'Where?' asks Toffee Cat.

'I don't know. Let's walk along this wall and find out.'

'I don't like dogs. Are they big dogs?' asks Toffee Cat.

'One is a brown dog. Brown dogs aren't big. Are they?' I ask.

'They might be,' Toffee Cat tells me.

'The white ones are small ones. Or is that the sheep in the field? Hmm.'

'The sheep are bigger than us,' I say. 'One dog is called Brandi and the other is called Rocky.'

'How do you know that?' Toffee Cat asks.

'Cos the telephone told Jade and Jade told me.'

'Okay. Let's walk,' says Toffee Cat.

I walk in front and we jump up onto a wall and walk along the top. It's not long before we can smell dog. I slow down to look down at a brown dog and Toffee Cat hits me in my bum.

'Watch it!' I say to Toffee Cat. 'I nearly fell of the wall then.'

'You didn't tell me you were going to slow down so I kept walking and accidentally bumped into you.'

'You should be looking where you are going,' barks a brown dog.

I quickly look down at him, and my tail becomes very bushy. This happens when I am afraid.

'Who are you?' I ask.

'My name is Brandi Dog. What's yours?'

'I am Chatty Cat and this is Toffee Cat,' I say.

'Who's that next to you?' I ask.

'I am Rocky, the cute one.'

'Hello Rocky, the cute one,' I say.

'Hello Rocky, the cute one,' says Toffee Cat.

'His name is Rocky Dog. Silly,' barks Brandi Dog.

'We know that, we were just joking,' laughs Toffee Cat.

'Okay. Ha. Ha,' says Brandi Dog. 'Where are you going?'

'For a stroll. You want to come along?' I ask.

'Only if you can unlock the gate,' says Rocky Dog.'

I look down at the gate. It has a big bolt across it.

'Too big for me to open. Too big for all of us to open.'

'Well that's it then. We're going to have to stay here,' says Brandi Dog to Rocky Dog.

'It's not that bad. We'll be going for our afternoon walk soon,' replies Rocky Dog.

'If you were a cat you could jump up onto this wall and come for a stroll,' I tell them.

'Yes, but we're not, are we?' says Brandi Dog.

'Of course not. You are dogs,' I reply.

'Come on Chatty Cat, let's go home for some food,' says Toffee Cat.

'Bye, Brandi Dog, bye, Rocky Dog,' I say, as I turn around and follow Toffee Cat home.

The Umbrella Thief

The next morning after breakfast Stray Cat and I are walking along the pavement. We've both got our tails in the air as we walk proudly, looking straight ahead.

'Oh no! You see what I see, Chatty Cat?' says Stray Cat.

'No, what's that?' I ask and I look to where Stray Cat is looking, towards the house where Bert the Parrot lives. And look, he's in the window, climbing up the blinds.

'He wants to work in a circus,' Stray Cat tells me.

'Oh,' I say.

'But his shehooman Katie won't let him go cos she loves him too much.'

'Oh,' I say again.

'I guess he's not coming out to play today,' says Stray Cat.

'We could ask him,' I say.

'He knows that we'll be under the umbrella if he wants to join us later. Come on, let's get there.'

It's not long before we see a pile of cats, but no umbrella.

We both stop and stare but we still can't see an umbrella. I wonder what's going on and I look to Stray Cat who's stood on my right side. He turns and looks at me. We're both looking at each other and I notice for the first time that he has cute eyes and a cute face. Could he be cuter than me? Could he?

'Stop staring at me. It's rude,' says Stray Cat.

'Is it?' I ask.

'Yes. Come on let's see what's happened to the umbrella.'

'Is there a cat umbrella thief?'

'Where?' Stray Cat asks me.

'I don't know. Anywhere.'

'Where is anywhere?' asks Stray Cat.

'I don't know. You walk a lot further than me and thought you would know.'

'I don't know.'

'Actually it wouldn't be a cat umbrella thief,' I say.

'Why not?' asks Stray Cat.

'Cos the umbrella would be too heavy for the cat umbrella thief to carry.'

'Oh yes. I didn't think of that,' says Stray Cat.

'It could be a hooman umbrella thief,' I say.

'Yes it could. Now come on, start walking.'

Saucepans in the Sky

When we arrive, Stray Cat looks around the group and asks, 'Where's Toffee Cat? He's usually here by now.'

'He's not here today cos he's on paw print duty,' says Sooty Cat.

'Paw print duty?' asks Stray Cat.

'What's that?'

'Toffee Cat waits outside the entrance to the police station in case they catch any cat burglars and they have their paw prints taken.'

'Oh,' says Stray Cat as he strolls over to the cats and lies down in his usual spot. 'I know Bert the parrot isn't coming as he's climbing up the blinds at home.'

'Oh,' says Sooty Cat.

'Oh,' says Clancy Cat.

I walk around them. I stop and then I walk around them again.

'What are you doing?' asks Clancy Cat.

'I'm looking to see if there is a hooman umbrella thief,' I say.

'Why?' asks Sooty Cat, before giving out a big yawn.

'Cos the umbrella is not here,' I say.

'Ah. The wind stole it,' says Sooty Cat.

'Why?' I ask.

'I don't know. The wind steals lots of things. Although I don't think the wind actually steals things. I think it's the wind's job to move things around without telling anyone.'

'Oh I see,' I say, and go and sit in my usual position.

'So why did it only take half of the stick which holds it up?'

'Perhaps it was a baby wind and not strong enough to take it out of the ground.'

'Ah, I see,' I say.

We are enjoying the warmth but the sun switch is not on so we're not hot-

hot and suddenly there's a big bang in the sky. BANG!

'Tut. Who is cooking in the sky and banging saucepans together?' I ask.

'I wonder why they're cooking up there?' says Sooty Cat looking up at the blue sky. 'My hooman cooks in the house.'

'And mine,' I say.

'They've stopped now,' says Sooty Cat.

'I don't like loud noises,' I say, 'Especially fireworks. They scare me.'

'And me,' I say.

'Where do you run to when the fireworks go off, Chatty Cat?'

'I run up the stairs, into the back bedroom, and under the bedside cabinet. Where do you hide, Sooty Cat?'

'Under the settee,' says Sooty Cat. 'Sometimes I'm okay.'

'Bert the Parrot likes thunder,' says Clancy Cat.

'When did he tell you that?' I ask.

'He didn't tell me. I read it on Pawbook.'

'Ah. I haven't been on there for a while. Jade signed me up for Pawbook but I can't remember which paw she said I had to use to 'sign in',' I say.

'It's your front left paw,' says Clancy Cat.

'What is?' I ask.

'The paw you use to sign into Pawbook.'

'Ah, thanks,' I say, and stare at a blade of grass in front of me.

A Kind Hooman

We all turn around when we hear some noise coming towards us. It's a big hehooman with big black shiny shoes and he's walking our way. We stare at him. I begin to arch my back to get ready to run if I need to but as he gets closer I can smell the leather from his shiny shoes and I want to rub my head on them.

'Hello, catty cats,' he says, and I look around to the cats and see that none of us is called catty cats. I hear the rustle of a bag and look up at the man. He's pulling a long pole out of his bag and suddenly Clancy Cat shouts, 'Run!' And we do, we run as fast as we can and all in different directions. We don't run far as luckily there are various things for us to hide behind. I'm behind a bin and I can see Clancy Cat and Sooty Cat are hiding in the bushes. But I can't see

Stray Cat. I hope he is okay, I know he will be okay as he knows how to look after himself. He is a streetwise cat.

I move to the corner of the bin so I can see what the hehooman is doing. He has put the pole that he took from his bag into the ground and oh, look, he's put a colourful umbrella on the top of it. It is nice, but that is our spot. I watch him a bit more and as I do I see Stray Cat coming out from under a car. Phew. Thank goodness he's safe. Though he shouldn't be anywhere near cars, that's dangerous.

Stray Cat tiptoes across the grass to get a better view of what the man is doing.

'Hello, you lovely cat,' says the hehooman to Stray Cat.

Stray Cat politely says, 'Hello' back.

'What's your name?' He asks.

'I'm not allowed to tell strangers my name or where I live.'

'Oh. Okay. You know I watch you cats every day and when I saw the wind had blown your umbrella away I went into the shed and got this old one out for you,' said hehooman.

'That is very nice of you. Thank you.' Stray Cat says to hehooman before meowing to the other cats that it's safe to come out of hiding. We all stroll along to where hehooman and Stray Cat are.

Stray Cat tells us what the man said about getting this umbrella for us out of his shed and I like him. I smile at him and then walk over to his shoes. I sniff them and then rub my head on them, first the left shoe then the right. Oooh, I do like leather.

I stop doing it when Stray Cat says to the hehooman, 'Why do you look at us from your window? Are you allowed to do that being an old man?'

Hehooman laughs and then says,

'It is wrong for men to look out of the window and stare at children but looking at cats is okay. I enjoy watching you cats come to the umbrella for your chats.'

'How do you know we chat if you are behind your window?' asks Sooty Cat.

'Ha ha. I watch your mouths move.' the hehooman tells us as he sits on the grass.

'What else do you do apart from look at us from your window?'

'I look after my dear wife, Doris.'

'Is she a shehooman?' asks Sooty Cat.

Laughing, hehooman says, 'Yes, she is a shehooman and she is my shehooman.'

'I have a shehooman and my shehooman is called Jade,' I say.

'I have one too and her name is Anne,' says Sooty Cat.

'My shehooman is called Mary,' says Clancy Cat.

We all look at Stray Cat. 'Your turn,' I say. 'What is the name of your shehooman?'

'I have lots of shehoomans and hehoomans,' says Stray Cat.

'Do you?' asks hehooman.

'Yes I do. When I am at Chatty Cat's house my shehooman's name is Jade and when I am at home my shehooman's name is Tina and my hehooman's name is Ben.'

Shehooman Doris

'Do you look after your shehooman Doris like my shehooman Jade looks after me?' I ask.

'Yes I do.'

'Even her toilet tray?' I ask.

'Well yes, sort of. My wife has dementia and is very ill and can't walk to the toilet so she uses a commode.'

'A commode?' enquires Sooty Cat.

'It's like a chair with a bed pan in the middle and my wife goes to the toilet in it and when she's finished I help her back to her chair and then wash out the bed pan.'

'What type of litter do you use?' I ask. 'I like the clumping stuff so shehooman Jade can scoop up my toilet and put it in the bin. Clancy Cat said that I should go to the toilet in the garden-room but sometimes it's too cold to go out as when I squat the wind blows up my bottom. He only wears his glasses when he chairs the Poop Group meetings.'

'Who does?' asks hehooman.

'Clancy Cat.'

'Oh,' says hehooman.

'What is dementsha?' asks Stray Cat.

'It's a brain disease that mainly older people get,' says hehooman.

'Is that when their hair turns white?' I ask.

'No, their hair doesn't always change colour as they get older. It doesn't affect everyone but there are a lot of people suffering with dementia.'

'What will happen to shehooman Doris?' I ask.

'The dementia kills off the brain cells and as time goes by she is unable to do things for herself. The disease has killed some of her brain so she cannot remember things she did recently, but she can remember things that happened a long time ago.'

I watch hehooman as he puts his hand into his pocket and pulls out a hanky and wipes his eyes. Hehooman is crying and I feel sad. I go over and sit by him and lick his hand. Then Stray Cat comes over and licks his other hand and Sooty Cat and Clancy Cat come over and sit by his legs.

'Can you remember what you had for your breakfast this morning?' hehooman asks me.

'Of course, I had meat and biscuits.'

'My Doris can't remember what she had for her breakfast because of the dementia.'

'I had meat and biscuits too,' says Sooty Cat.

'Doris had her favourite for breakfast, Weetabix, but she wouldn't remember if I asked her.' Hehooman looks at his watch on his wrist and says 'I'd better be going. Doris's carer will be going soon.' And he stood up, said goodbye and walked away.

'Thank you for the umbrella,' I say.

'You're welcome,' the hehooman says as he waves his hand in the air and walks off. I walk a little bit to see which way he is going. I may visit him one day and meet shehooman Doris.

Camera

The next day we're sat under the new umbrella.

'There's something different about this umbrella,' says Toffee Cat.

'Is there?' asks Clancy Cat.

'I noticed that,' says Bird the Parrot. 'It feels softer.'

Clancy Cat is laughing. 'What are you laughing at?' asks Bert the Parrot.

'You haven't noticed have you? The wind moved our umbrella and a hehooman came and gave us his.'

'That was nice of him,' says Bert the Parrot.

'Yes it was,' says Toffee Cat.

'Hey, Toffee Cat. Did you see any cat burglars at the police station yesterday?' asks Sooty Cat.

'No but I got some free food when I walked round to the fish market on my way home.'

'I go there sometimes,' says Stray Cat.

'Can we all go one day?' asks Bert the Parrot.

'Too many if we all go at once,' says Stray Cat.

'I wish Jade would stop taking photos of me. I am fed up with smiling for the camera, she even took one of me in cat prison. Look!'

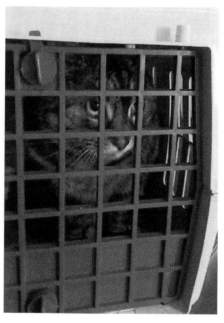

'Why were you in cat prison?' asks Clancy Cat.

'I wasn't really in cat prison, I went to the vet cos I had an allergy,' I say.

'This is me sticking my tongue out but I can't remember why,' says Toffee Cat.

'It was Fish-Friday and Anne my shehooman had not given me any fish so I stared at these instead,' says Sooty Cat.

'What are your fish called?' asks Toffee Cat.

'Fish One and Fish Two,' replies Sooty Cat.

'How do you know which is Fish One and which is Fish Two?'

'That's easy. Fish One is the first one that comes to me,' says Sooty Cat.

'I like to climb up the blinds in the window, stay there for a little while and then climb back down again. It's fun!' says Bert the Parrot.

My shehooman Mary caught me on Pawbook the other day. Look!'

'And me!' I say.

And we all mew (laugh).

By myself

I've had a busy time meeting all my new friends and today I am going to take it easy and stay in my garden-room and have a rest. I go and sit in my jungle. Just me and a few insects climbing up the leaves.

I start thinking of the tortoises, Om and Daenerys, and wonder what they are doing. I decide to go and visit them and find out.

Walking along the wall I stop by the house where Rocky Dog and Brandi Dog live. They're not in the garden-room and I wait for them to come out. I am still waiting so I jump down onto the grass and I see a note on the garden table. It says that they've gone out.

've gone out for a walk. DO NO
our house. Repeat. DO NOT ro
r house. We'll be back later.
you are leaving us food please p
in our Dog Den aka the she
ank you.
      Rocky Dog and Brandi Dog

I jump back up onto the wall and make my way to where the tortoises live. When I run out of wall I jump onto the fence. It hurts my paws but I walk along it and then jump down to where the tortoises are.

'Hello, Torts. I would call you by your names if I knew how to tell the difference between you both.'

'That's easy. My name is Om and my nose is round. I like cucumber.'

'And my name is Daenerys, my nose is more pointed and I love red lettuce,' he says as he starts walking towards me.

He stops by my front paw, my right one, and 'Ouch! You just bit my paw!' I walk away and he follows me. I jump down the steps.

'You got bunny rabbit feet,' says Daenerys.

'I do not,' I tell him.

'You do, too.'

'How can I have bunny rabbit feet if I am a cat?'

'I don't know. You need to ask your shehooman,' says Om.

'Perhaps you're a bunny cat,' says Daenerys.

I lift my front right paw and look at it.

'It's a cat paw,' I say. I do the same with my left front paw. 'And this one is a cat's paw too.'

'It's your back paws that are bunny rabbit feet,' says Daenerys.

'They are not,' I say.

'They are when you jump down steps with your back paws together.'

'Well I won't jump down steps then,' I say. I start walking and Om is following me. He is trying to bite my tail so I raise it up.

I walk over to the wall and squat down ready to jump up onto the fence.

'Don't go, we're only having fun,' says Daenerys.

'I need to go home. It's nearly feed-me time,' I tell him.

When I get home I find Jade in the kitchen. The sun is shining through the window, I am hot and I throw myself onto the floor.

'Why are you cooking meat? It's Fish-Friday.' I say.

'I know but we haven't got any fish,' Jade tells me.

'But it's Fish Friday!' I tell Jade.
'We still haven't got any.'

Little Cat

I am sitting under the umbrella with Toffee Cat, Sooty Cat, Stray Cat and Clancy Cat. Bert the Parrot is on his spot on top of the umbrella.

'I love lazing here on the grass but I do have a question for you, Bert,' I say as I stretch my front paws out.

'Do you?' says Bert.

'Yes I just said I did,' I tell him.

'Go on then, what's your question?'

'Why don't you fly off?'

'Fly off? Where to?'

'Anywhere.'

'Why would I want to go anywhere? Where is anywhere anyway?'

'Ha ha, Bert. I think Chatty Cat means why you stay on the umbrella, usually birds fly away.'

'Why would I want to fly away when my friends are here?'

'Good answer Bert,' says Clancy Cat as he raises his head from the ground, looks around and lays back down again. His head isn't down for long until he raises it again. I stand up and look at what he's looking at.

Two cats are walking towards us, and it looks like the little one is being chased by the big white one. Both have their tails up straight and bushy like brushes, showing they are angry. I look at Clancy Cat and then to Stray Cat and then to Sooty Cat and then to Toffee Cat, all are stood up staring at these two cats coming towards us. The little one is running, running towards us. His running is getting faster.

'Help me. Help me!' screams the little cat.

'Get out of the way. He's got fleas, need to run him out of town,' shouts the big white cat.

'Purrlease help me! Purrlease! He keeps attacking me,' says the little cat.

Stray Cat walks up to the little cat and says, 'We will protect you. Stand behind Chatty Cat, Toffee Cat and Sooty Cat. Bert the Parrot, Clancy Cat and I will go and talk to White Cat.'

Little Cat does as he's told and stands behind us but it's not long before he is sat on the grass scratching his neck with his back right paw. I turn and watch as the cats stroll up to White Cat, with Bert hitching a ride on Stray Cat's back. White Cat arches his back ready to pounce on them.

'Hey relax, we're not here to hurt you. We just want to know why you're chasing Little Cat.'

'I told you, he's got fleas.'

'Yes but that's no reason to be horrible to him. It's not his fault.'

'Who's fault is it then?'

'His hooman's, of course. They should put that cold stuff on his neck every month.'

'I used to prefer the flea collar but now I have the cold stuff too,' says Clancy Cat.

Little Cat is meowing as he scratches the itchy bits on his skin. He hasn't got much fur. It reminds me of when I was a stray and I got fleas and I itched so much I lost my fur and my skin was all scabby.

'I will look after you, Little Cat. Come with me,' I say.

'Where we going?'

'I'm going to take you home and I will ask my shehooman Jade to tell the telephone that Jenny needs to come to the house and tell us how to get rid of your fleas.'

'Who is Jenny?' Little Cat asks before sitting down and scratching himself again.'

'Jenny rescued me from the streets and treated my fleas and my scabs.'

'Will she like me?'

'Of course she will.'

'White Cat didn't like me cos I am different.'

'You are not different. You are the same as us. Well not the same as Bert the Parrot cos he's a Parrot but you're the same as us cats.'

'Am I?' he says and stops and looks at me.

'Yes you are. Come on, this is my house.'

We lower ourselves under the gate and walk up the path to the door. I run into the house.

'Jade! Jade! Quick, tell the telephone that Jenny needs to come and look at Little Cat.'

'Little Cat?' asks Jade.

'Yes, come and meet Little Cat.'

Jade comes out into my Garden-room.

'Hello Little Cat. I won't stroke you as your skin looks sore. Let me go and get the telephone.'

Jade walks back into the house and I go and sit on the grass near Little Cat.

'Where do you live?'

'I am homeless. I used to have a house but my hoomans moved away and didn't take me with them.'

I smell food and look over and see Jade coming out with a dish. It smells like my food but there's only one dish, and for once I don't mind going without.

'Little Cat can have this food, Jade.'

'You are so caring, Chatty Cat,' says Jade.

'Thank you, Chatty Cat,' says Little Cat.

'I was a stray once, so lonely and hungry and now look at me, I have a house, a slave and you can stay in my Cat Den tonight if you want to.'

'Ooh, yes please. Thank you, Chatty Cat.'

We look by the gate as Stray Cat comes under it.

'Thank you for getting the cat away from me, Stray Cat,' says Little Cat.

'That's okay. We do not like Bully Cats,' says Stray Cat as he walks back down the garden path. 'Whether you are a bird, a cat, a child or an adult you must not bully people.'

'Where you going, Stray Cat?' I ask.

'Little Cat will need to use the Cat Den this evening. I'll pop home and say hello to my hoomans, I haven't seen them for a while.'

There's a knock on the front door and I run through the house and sit on the stairs to see who it is.

Ah, it's Jenny. I run down the stairs straight to Jenny and meow,

'Quick come on, Jenny, come and treat Little Cat.'

Jenny follows me out into the garden-room and goes over to Little Cat who is licking the empty dish. She picks him up and says, 'Poor you. Let's make you better. I'm going to take you home. You poor thing.' And she puts him into a little carrier and walks out of the front door.

'Bye, Little Cat,' I say.

'Bye, Chatty Cat, thank you.'

When Jade closes the front door I say,

'What will Jenny do with Little Cat?'

'The same as she did for you. She will look after him, give him some medicine and look for his owner. Probably put his picture on Facebook hoping that someone knows him.'

'Will she put it on Pawbook too?'

Jade bends down and strokes me, 'Yes, it will be on Pawbook too.'

'Can you remind me of my pawword so I can get on Pawbook and see him?'

'Yes, later, after you've had your food. Come on.'

It's a long time since I had my food and I have finished my food and I am waiting for Jade to get off Facebook and help me get onto Pawbook.

Pawbook

I'm bored. Bored. Bored. Bored. I look over at Jade who is sat with the laptop on her lap. I go over and head butt her right leg. She ignores me. I stroll through the house and casually walk up the stairs to my room. I jump up onto my bed and then up onto the windowsill where my laptop is. I press all the keys until I get onto Pawbook.

Chatty Cat

Chat here I forgot which paw to use for my pawword so I pressed them all and look! I'm on line.

Bert the Parrot.

Chat here Good to see you, Chatty Cat.

Clancy Cat

Chat here Hello Chatty Cat. I'm now going to get some food.

Chatty Cat

Chat here Okay. I will too.

Cat and Mouse

I'm walking along the fence and then the wall. I look ahead and I can see Stray Cat with something on his back. I walk a bit closer and I can see more clearly now. Ah, that must be Charlie Mouse on Stray Cat's back. He's pressing the button to stop the traffic so they can cross the road.

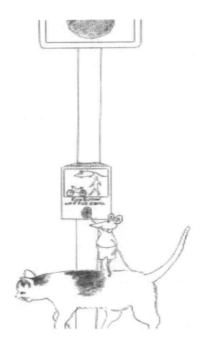

I decide to go and join them. I walk quickly along the wall then jump down and walk as fast as I can.

'Hello Stray Cat,' I say, puffing as I'm out of breath.

'Hello Chatty Cat. This is Charlie Mouse.'

'Hello Charlie Mouse,' I say looking at him. I don't usually see mice stood on the back of a cat.

'Hello Chatty Cat.' He says as jumps off of Stray Cat.

'I have to go now. See you another time,' says Charlie mouse.

'Bye, Charlie Mouse,' says Stray Cat.

'Bye, Charlie Mouse,' I say.

We watch Charlie Mouse run away into the bushes.

'Can I have a sleep over at your house tonight, Chatty Cat?' Stray Cat asks.

'Course you can, in the Cat Den,' I tell him.

And later that night I look out of the window before I go to bed and I see Stray Cat asleep in the Cat Den.

'Night night, Stray Cat.' x

Stories by young hoomans who have been inspired by Chatty Cat's books

Micky's Cat Party

On the 6th of June, Micky the cat wanted to have a party because it was her birthday. She had six weeks to plan her party. The first week she decided on where it was going to be. The second week she made all the colourful and glittery decorations. The third week she placed all the decorations where they were supposed to be. The fourth week she bought all the ingredients to make all the yummy food and all the party games. The fifth week she went down the road to invite all her cat friends. She asked Chatty Cat, Maggie, Buster, Poppy and Pete if they wanted to come to her party. Finally, on the sixth week she made all the yummy food. She had loads of fun making it all. Everything had gone so well, she just wished the party was fun, fun, fun.

All her lovely cat friends were happy to join her to celebrate her birthday. They all walked to her house. While they were walking to the house they could hear the music going "don't stop the party". So of course they were singing and dancing by the time they got there.

They went through the house into the back garden, when they stepped outside they saw all the yummy food, there was cat cake made with ham, cucumber slices, cat milk ice lollies, sausages and of course cat treats. The bouncy castle and all the other fun games were ready to be played with. Micky said, above the noise of the music, "Let's party."

The first thing they did was to eat the cat treats, yummy. After that they bounced on the bouncy castle and played pin the tail on the dog. Everyone was having so much fun. After hours of fun it was time for the ham cake. They all sang Happy Birthday and ate the delicious cake.

When Micky went inside to get the party bags she noticed that it was 6 o'clock in the afternoon and so they all had to go home as most owners like to have their cats home to sit with in the evening. So Micky went to take all her friends home and thank them for making her day super special. When she came back home she sat with her family and finished eating her yummy cake, opened her presents and played with a few of them. What an amazing day it had been, everyone had so much fun.

Then she lay in her bed cuddling her new fluffy and soft kitty who she named Tatty Kitty. It had been hard work planning it but oh so worth it. Can't wait for next year. She fell asleep happy with her day.

©Emily
Hummel

Lost:
Good or Bad?

Every day, I go outside. It's one of my favourite things to do. Otherwise, I am a pain for everyone and I'll complain loads until I get told for about the third time to be quiet (this is normally between 3 - 6 o'clock in the morning). Anyway, when I first went outside, the furthest that I went was about a quarter way down the garden. However, I have grown and become older. So, I've now started to go further down the garden, in the front garden, and near the roads.

One day, my family went out and by the looks of things, they weren't going to be back until the afternoon... if not evening. Therefore, I ate a bit of food and went outside - as usual. I went out of my little door and then looked through the gate to see whether my family's car was still there. They were just leaving. I waited until they had turned the corner.

"YES!! I can do whatever I want without being watched by Mum! Mm...what first?" I thought. "I know! I can wander further down the road." I jumped up onto the garden chairs, then the huge bin, then the near-on destroyed shed, then the roof of our next door neighbour's garage, and finally I jumped down onto the bins and onto the ground. I was in the front garden at last. I walked out to the path that was next to where Dad parks his car. When they go out, I can turn right without getting told off. So I did so.

On the way, I passed six houses and when I nearly crossed the seventh, these two big dogs started to bark loudly at me! They were bashing against the gate that held them away from me! I was like lightning! FLASH! GONE! Down the alleyway which was in-between the sixth and seventh house. I eventually felt safe enough to stop.

Where am I? Which way did I come from? Are those dogs gone? The questions kept on coming. I was lost.

Once I realised that no one was here, I started to try and figure out which way I came. All I wanted to do was to cry and have Megan or Mum or any member of my family come and stroke me and wake me up from a bad dream. But this wasn't going to be the case. I wandered around to see if there was anyone who could tell or show me the way home. After a little while, I realised that I wasn't getting anywhere near the familiar path that I had once been on before. I passed several tempting mice. But I decided to not chase them. I just wanted my home. Besides, I was still worn out by running from those dogs and I didn't feel in the mood to chase three little mice. I wanted to find a fellow cat that could lead me back onto the familiar path. Or maybe a bit further down so that I'm with someone when we pass those dogs.

About 30 minutes later, I started to give up. I was exhausted. I thought that I was far enough from danger. I curled up and went to sleep...

"*Help! These big dogs are chasing me and I can't shake them off! Help! Someone please!*"

"*Are you crazy!? We aren't going to get caught up in that! You're mental!!*"

"*Please! Help!*"

"Hello! Are you ok? Not many cats sleep here."

"Sleep? I'm not sleeping, I'm being chased!" There was a tap on me. I jumped and opened my eyes just to see another cat standing right in front of me.

"Trust me. You're not being chased. You're fine."

"Oh, sorry."

"My name is Alexa. What is yours?"

"My name is Micky."

"Hi Micky." She gave me a warm, friendly smile that reminded me of the smile that I get from my family. "Are you ok?"

"Well...not really. I got frightened by these big dogs and I forgot to keep track of where I was going. I got lost."

"Oh no!"

"Do you think that you could lead me back to the alleyway between two houses?"

"Of course! But...I was on my way to a cat concert. Would you like to come?"

"Yes please!"

"Great! By the way, 'Cat Direction' and 'Little Meow' will be there!"

"Cool!! I can't wait!!"

We headed towards the concert and I completely forgot that I was lost. When we arrived, Cat Direction were on the stage and were about to sing.

"Do you like them?" asked Alexa.

"Of course! They are two of my favourites!"

We continued to party and dance to both Cat Direction's and Little Meow's songs. I was having a great time.

After a while, I looked up and it was dark.

"Alexa, is it possible if you can take me to that alleyway now? My family will be back soon and they'll be worried sick if I'm not home when they come."

"Of course I can. By the way, you make a really good friend. Do you wanna meet tomorrow?"

"Um...what about you come to mine? I don't think that I want to get lost again tomorrow," I replied.

"Yes, that'll be fun!" Alexa answered.

Alexa led me back to the familiar path - the dogs were in their house so that was a relief.

"Anyway, see you tomorrow."

"Ok. See you then. Thank you for everything."

"It's a pleasure. Anytime," Alexa said sweetly. I waved goodbye and started to trot back to my house. Whilst doing this, a blue car pulled up. They're back! They're home! Mum opened the door and said:

"Why are you still outside at this time of night?" I simply replied with an innocent "meow" and everyone started to smile. I followed them all back to the house, finished my food, then followed everyone upstairs. After today and Alexa, is being lost good or bad?

©Megan Hummel

Gangster Cat

I recently just moved to my new house. Oh, by the way, I am Maggie! The other day I set out for the first time and while I was walking along I bumped into a large cat.

I said, 'Oops, sorry.'

'Wait, I am Gangster Cat. What's your name?' he asked in a croaky voice.

'Erm... my name's Maggie,' I whispered.

'Say it louder,' shouted Gangster Cat.

'My name is Maggie,' I squealed.

'Fine. Follow me,' said Gangster Cat.

So I followed him 'cause, you know, he looks like a yellow cat. He led me to a theme park obstacle course and all of it was full of cats.

'Try level one,' said Gangster Cat.

'Erm...' I whispered.

'Maggie!' shouted my family.

'Sorry, gotta go,' I said. 'Erm. Where are we?'

Gangster Cat walked to my house with me and left within a flash, so I just started meowing at the front door and soon enough Ruby let me in and picked me up, fed me, put me to bed. 'Zzzzzzz,' I snored.

I woke up and woke mum and Ruby up. I left Euan in peace because he doesn't like being woken up. I went downstairs, had my breakfast and headed out to see Gangster Cat.

'Maggie, you returned,' said Gangster Cat.

'I had no choice, 'cause of you,' I said.

'Yes you did!' shouted Gangster Cat.

'Ok I did,' I whispered.

Because I was working all day and my family didn't know I was gone, I reached level two, yay!

We had a celebration but not that much. Cats came and the DJ was there and there was a sign saying 'Mini Gangster Cat'.

'Well done, Maggie. Sorry that not many cats have come,' Gangster Cat Said.

There were five cats there, me, Gangster Cat, Molly (my next door neighbour's cat), Chatty Cat (my other next door neighbour's cat), and Micki (my yellow cat).

I heard a bark and it was a lost dog after us so we ran and everything got knocked over by the dog. We hid in Micki's back garden and fell asleep there.

When I woke up Gangster Cat walked me home again. I had breakfast and headed out again.

Level two took a while to complete because we had to get the park back to normal.

At the end of the week I completed it and now I am the best cat ever and now I am at level 53 and took over all the other cats' levels, and now I protect every cat (including Gangster Cat) and

every cat comes to my celebration parties.
My family are very proud of me.

©Ruby Ashman

Paws for Thought...

What must hoomans consider if they are thinking of getting a cat/kitten?

We cost money!

We are for life! We will be with you for a long time. Many, many years hopefully.

We need:

Regular flea and worming treatment
Annual vaccinations
Neutering/spaying (if pregnancy is not wanted)
Micro-chipping in case we get lost

Things you need to buy for the cat/kitten (if you haven't already got them)

Litter, litter tray and tray liners (tray liners optional). Having a hood for the tray is good but how will you know when it needs changing? Will your cat fit in it with a hood on? Will your cat feel claustrophobic?
Wet food e.g. tinned food
Dry food e.g. biscuits
Scratching post
Toys e.g. balls, cardboard, soft toys etc.
Collar, bell and disc with phone number on it (optional)

We also need:
Somewhere to sleep. Can we sleep on the furniture? On your bed?

We love the feel of carpet and we like to sleep on it sometimes. If you have laminate flooring, this is good in the summer but we also need a bit of carpet, too. Jade has laminate flooring in her office and I have a bath mat in there to sleep on. And in the lounge she has laminate flooring but, luckily, she has a carpet in the middle of the room, which I sit on, and sleep on, now and again.

We need company, now and again. Personally, I don't like to be stroked all the time, unless I'm on Jade's lap, but I do like her to be there when I come back after I've had a busy day outside.

Stimulation, now and again. If we get bored, we scratch furniture and carpets.

To be told what is acceptable and what isn't, but be careful how and when you do this as the cat or kitten is just settling in. Telling it off or making demands on it can cause it a lot of harmful stress.

Dear Reader

If you have enjoyed reading about my journey from being homeless to having my own house, then please tell your friends and relatives and leave a review on Amazon.
Thank you.

I have my own Facebook page and blog, and many followers. You can follow me on

Facebook:
https://www.facebook.com/ChattyCat?ref_type=bookmark

Twitter: @chattycatsuzi

Blog:
http://chattycatno1.wordpress.com/

The Author

Internationally selling author, Suzan Collins, enjoys writing fiction as it allows her to make up stories - and eat cake! She also writes non-fiction to inform others - and eats cake!

To see all books by Suzan Collins and find out more about her, please visit:
Website: www.suzancollins.com
Facebook Author page:
http://goo.gl/zfiqyv
Twitter: @suzancollins

Books in the Chatty Cat series

Chatty Cat: My Purr-fect New Home
ISBN 978-0-9954844-3-6

Chatty Cat: Spring into Summer
ISBN 978-0-9934934-4-7

Chatty Cat: My Purr-fect Friends
ISBN 978-0-9934934-5-4

Release date: July 2016
Chatty Cat: Activity Book
ISBN 978-0-9934934-9-2

Release date: Feb 2017
Chatty Cat: Autumn into Winter
ISBN 978-0-9934934-8-5

Love

Chatty Cat

xx

Printed in Great Britain
by Amazon